MW01419397

Confessions of

a Homebound Prodigal

Russ Brunn

For my parents

and my grandparents,

for giving me the greatest gift of all:

the gift of faith —

and for always leaving

the light on for me

prodigal

:

one who spends money

or resources freely and

recklessly

The older son never left his father's house but was never close to his father's heart. The younger son wandered far away from his father's house and squandered everything that had been given to him—

but it was his heart that drew him back after his wandering was over.

The Gospel of Luke 15:11-32

We are all prodigals.

We are all wanderers. Every one of us at some point has made a choice to set out on a journey that was not in our Father's best plan for us, to squander what did not belong to us; but He didn't stop us. In fact, He sent us out with the inheritance we asked for. He blessed us and kept the light on for our return.

Every one of us has sat in that pig pen and felt the ache of longing to be back in a place of purpose, of safety and security, a place of love and acceptance and perfect peace. We each remember the moment when we first lifted our head and turned our face toward home again.

Most of these confessions and meditations were written from that place of turning, and while making that journey home. They depict and chronicle the struggle and faith of one wanderer who decided that his 'freedom' wasn't worth it—that his Father was right—and that he wanted to be home again.

My prayer is that you will find yourself in these pages, that you will see yourself walking that long dusty road back to the Father as you echo the questions, prayers, and confessions that have flowed from my own heart—

and most of all that as you turn these pages you will find yourself getting closer to home.

Contents

Seven

the best seven words,
the truest prayer
i've said in a long time:

you are right
and
i am wrong

Undeserved

I am the woman
in the middle of the crowd,
all the stones aimed at her…

I am the stubborn,
fruitless tree of which you said:

dig around it and let it have
one more year of
undeserved,
highly abused,
never-ending grace

Beckoning

Grace says
come just one step
and I'll come a million miles
to meet you

Love says
give me just
the soles of your feet
and I'll put
a crown on your head

Evergreen

Towels won't dry in the wintertime,
the same way wounds won't shut
flowers won't grow
coughs and colds won't let up
and hearts won't heal.

We need some South

some warm
some grace and a window
that stays open.

We are all longing for the Sun.

Remind Me

that you want to feed
the multitudes
with my broken pieces

Patience

The Sun is a patient and uncomplaining lover.
It does not lie—
You can't say it doesn't give ample warning.

It lends you only so many glorious months
for savoring, and then one day,
like an exploited heart, it starts taking back
warmth and light, little by little,
hour by minute, forcing you into
hooded sweatshirts, heated cars, and early nights:

Now it is your turn for patience.

You know it will come back around again
to knock at your door and sit at your table.

You know it while you rake the leaves
and shovel the snow.

You know it as you address Christmas cards
and add blankets to your bed.

Still, there is such a fine line between
knowing and believing.

Stir

An empty page
What will it be
Pain, fear, regret or rage
All the things that crowd
the empty space inside of me

A life of sin
A twisted destiny
Where do I begin
What are you asking of me

A tattered warrior
A jaded heart
A weary traveler
Not quite sure where to start

A bruised conscience
A weathered flame
Begging for a second chance
Waiting for you to give me a new name

A repentant son
A forgiving father
Meeting at last
Here at the altar

A heart full of questions
An abundance of answers
Stir my spirit, move my tired feet
Give meaning to my soul
Like rhythm to a dancer

The Same Sun

Where exactly does repentance begin?
If you were to draw a line on the ground,
which blade of grass first caught the scent of it
as it made its way toward you—
which piece of earth was the first to touch it
as it passed by?

I think of it more as dream than a moment—
something like sleep that over takes you
without your full awareness of it

But when you wake up,
you know something's changed,
and you won't be the same, because
you're certainly not where you were before

I think of it like the afternoon Sun
drying a rock after a heavy rain.
Who can tell the moment the rock is
completely dry?

All you know is that it is dry, and hot,
and reflecting heat back to the Sun—

and you know,
because you have seen it happen before,
that when it rains again, the same Sun
will come out from behind the same clouds
to dry all the rocks
and warm everyone around

and grow all the flowers
and start all the fires
that can never be put out

Faith

Faith is
letting go of something
and watching it die
without trying to revive it
believing that
after death has occurred,
God, the giver and source
of all life,
will bring back to life
in its place
something of incomparable value
to the thing you first dared
to let go of.

Bridges

there are hearts
that need reconciling

letters that should be
postmarked and sent

phone calls to be made

spaces that need some thread
just a little bit of cable

to pull them back together
again

there are words I need you to hear

but the canyon is much too dark
i have only so many hands

and you are much too far way
to see them waving now

have your way

i look at this hole
in the ground
the hole
that has been dug for me
i look at these dead things
in my hands
these dead things
that have been killing me
i look at my master
standing beside
this grave
standing beside me
and i know
it is time
my friends
time for death
time for goodbye
time for open hands
time for a hundred and eighty

i know it is time for death
because it is the nature
of my master
to declare first dead
and then alive
the things that
do not fit me anymore
the things that
have become too big
for my hands to hold
and so in his mercy
out of the storehouses of his grace
my master
has dug this grave for me
and all he asks

is that i leave the dead things
in the ground

i look at my master
and see that his hands
are full too
of things
that he wants to give me
but he can only hand them to me
as i let go of the things
that i have already filled
my hands with

i hear a faint song
and find my own voice
rising to join the chorus
as i extend my fingers
to bare my open palms
finally emptied
of the things i grasped
and clung tightly to
for so long

and standing here
beside this hole
beside my master
i begin to sing loudly
and boldly
the song that is saving my life:

"Come death with your sting
Come death, for i know
it is life that you bring
Come death and do not delay
Precious Jesus have your way
Yes, have your way with me…"

I Can't Help It

I can't help but be moved
by the empty cardboard box
laying lifeless in the lot next door,
at the mercy of the wind,
the rising and falling temperatures—

an old man having lived out his purpose,
having been filled and emptied again,
waiting to be recycled, burned, pressed down,
torn apart and put back together again
in the form of something else, something
completely different beyond his control.

I can't help but think of my life
like that box, at the mercy of so many things
like time and prejudice.

I can't help but wonder if I will be laying
there on my side all poured out, exposed
and empty, after my life is done —
after the good has been sucked out of me,
an abandoned shell aching for the storehouse,
a frame longing for the shelter it once was.

Prayer of Expectation

What will it take
To get me to where I need to be
What do you want, God
What are you asking of me

A tiny spark
A raging fire
A step of faith
A moment of desire

Something drastic
Something simple
Something permanent
Something useful

To help me move this mountain
To help me get over this wall
And find what I am looking for
When I seek after you most of all

Tell me to go, and I will go
Tell me to stay, and I will stay
Just tell me what you want me to do
Speak to me, Father, and I will obey

shallow end

i've resisted the deep end
and have painted pictures
in the shallow

I've Got

a bike I never ride
a shelf of books I never read
a God I never pray to:

a jar full of aging seed

What Am I To Do

What am I to do
With these memories
That won't stop
Burning holes in me

What am I to do
With these hands
That I am afraid of now
For they know far too much

What am I to do
With this identity
Is this really who I am
Or who I was trying to be

What am I to do
With this jaded soul
Tell me what can I do
I just want to be made whole

What am I to do
With all this sin
Do I dare to believe
That you could wash me clean again

What am I to do
With everything that I know
With my eyes open so wide
Where am I to go

What am I to do
With things I do not understand
And cannot begin to comprehend
What am I to do with them

What am I to do
With this enormous pride
That blocks out the light
And makes me cold inside

What am I to do
With this paralyzing fear
Where did I go wrong
And how did I end up here

What am I to do
God, what should I do
I only ask you these things because
I want to know You
And be more like You

Show me your will, Father
Tell me what am I to do

runaway train

there are things in my hands
that need to go
things in my heart
that need to be demolished
crushed
broken
and sown
but it is so much easier
to cling to a seed
than to let it fall
into the cruel earth
an earth that does not lie
an earth that promises a good return
on the things we lament and mourn

there are things in my head
that need to stop
things in my soul
that need to be put to rest
laid down
chained
and silenced
but it is far more comforting
to keep replaying the scenes
that feed my ravenous flesh
than to lay them under the knife
and watch them drift away
in little tiny pieces

there are things in my life
that need to change
things in my person
that need to be turned around
inside out
upside down

back to a place of order
and relief
but it is far easier
to wish on the star
that used to shine so bright
instead of putting my last dollar
on the runaway train
that is just about to pass me by

Letter from Home

The oak floor misses you,
your strong back,
and the way you would sit
leaning up against the wall
all afternoon long

The circle has two less hands now,
the table one less chair

The walls still ask about you
The hall upstairs
creaks your name late at night

And sometimes, every once in awhile,
I swear the moon comes
out of hiding with its brilliant spotlight
to search for you

We all miss you now and then:

the front steps, and the back field.
the trees, the swing, the holidays,
and Saturday mornings

But of all these things, I think
the music misses you the most

what good is

what is life
if not a battle
and what good is a battle
without the will to fight

how strong are the sidelines
but how cruel
are the excuses
that keep a warrior
on the bench
in the safety
in the clear
on fragile hinges
under a pregnant sky

how bitter the tears
in the calm of night
shed by the safe and secure
no blood on their courage
no mountains under their feet
how silent the dreams
caged in regret
that lay soothed and suffocated
under terrified ribs

'do not fear'
he said to me
'be strong and very courageous
and do not fear'
yet all the while
it is fear I have clung to
and hidden behind
to make the most
of what I think is real
instead of letting go

instead of trusting
to find a reality
that will last
a future
that won't betray me
or lie to me
the way i lie to myself

what is a life
if there is no death
no dying
no giving up or giving in
but only a holding on
what a tragic grip it is
that holds me
that i cling to
these faces, these memories
none of which can save me

my own death would be my salvation
the closing of my own eyes
would bring the most light
and yet still I stare
into what's blinding me
still I cling
to what's devastating me
etching the life
right out of me

what good is faith
without something unseen
and how good is a void
if you're always trying to fill it
instead of letting it be
letting something come to you
something that you can receive
gratefully

humbly
and not take all the credit for
instead of a house
that you built around yourself
four little walls to remind you
that you made it all on your own
what good are those walls
that look more like
prison bars
from the inside

what good is one more chance
if you never take it
how deep can mercy run
if you always run from it
and how far can forgiveness reach
when you only slap the hand
that tries to save you,
shame the face
that gave you your own name

what is life
if not a battle
and what good is a battle
without the will to fight

Sad Stories

Write about love,
You say
About sunshine
And flowers
And happy endings

And I look up
From my tragedy
And tell you
I can only write
What I know
I can only tell
What I have heard
I can only press into
The life that I have lived
And beg others
Not to repeat
My sad, sad stories

The Valley
Hebrews 13:5
Psalm 23:4

i hear
the valley
calling out your name
it's calling your name
not mine
but i will go there with you
i will walk beside you
and i will never leave you
or forsake you
i will brave the dark
for your light
i will have faith
for your fight
i will hold my head up
for your courage
i will take another step
for your destination

i see
the road
beckoning you
it's beckoning your feet
not mine
but i will go there with you
i will walk beside you
and i will never leave you
or forsake you
when you are too tired
i will offer you my shoulder
when you are too weak
i will be your rest
when you can't see anymore
i will be your eyes

when you can't take another step
i will carry you

i see
the cross
ahead of you
there on the mountain
it's your cross
not mine
but i will go there with you
i will walk beside you
and i will never leave you
or forsake you
i will pick up your cross
and put it on my back
i will take your thorns
and place them on my head
i will hold your burden
in my hands
i will put your pain
in my heart
if only to answer
your deepest questions
your loudest cry of:
"what is love"
i will speak
but not with words
and i will tell you of this love
and if you can't see me
if you can't feel me
there beside you
if you can't hear me
then i will tell you again
and again
and again
i will never stop speaking of
this love

this love i have for you
until you reach the top of the hill
and lay your burden down
and let me nail it to the cross
that i have carried for you

i hear
the valley
calling out your name
it's calling your name
not mine
but i will go there with you
i will walk beside you
and i will never leave you
or forsake you

I Am Small

because I have let you be
my Savior
but not my King

I am shallow
because I have taken
your Grace
but not your discipline

I am ashamed
because instead of
taking up my own cross
like you asked me to
I have carelessly
walked all over yours

This Is My Love

What is it, you ask,
That made me walk down this path
What is it, you wonder
That made me want to live this way
I stare at you blankly
And I don't know what to say
How can I make you understand

I never chose this life
I never chose this pain
I never chose this disillusionment
I was thrown into something
That was out of my control from the very start
I was forced to deal with my feelings
And experiences
And beliefs
The very best way I knew how

So who are you to judge
How can you ever know
What you would have chosen
If you were never given a choice either
Maybe you would have been me
And I could have been you

You tell me God loves me
Just like he loves you
You tell me this
But I can't hear you
Because I don't know what love is

Your love is marriage
Your love is perfect unity
One man and one woman for life
A husband and a wife
Two kids and a car
A house and a dog
A fence and a mailbox
That is your life
That is your love
That is your pat on the back

My love is selfish
My love is obsession and addiction
My love gives and gives without getting anything back in return
It reaches and reaches
My love tries a little bit harder
Just one more time
Before it collapses

My love is relentless
My love is futile
My love is empty
My love is resentment
It is bitter and unlucky
My love is crowded bars
Tight jeans
Sweat on the dance floor
Cigarettes by the back door
My love is waiting and waiting
For someone who will never call
Laying in bed tossing and turning

Wondering where I went wrong
My love is passed out drunk on the floor
Selfishness that cannot be explained
Only returned
This is my life
This is my love
This is the knife in my back

This is the only love I have ever known
So call it what you will
God loves me and God loves you
And I have yet to know
What love is

this knowledge

i watch from the corner
from my quiet, miserable perch
i listen
and my heart bleeds
for myself
and all the other men
whose hearts know things
that their hearts
and their bodies
their schedules
and their tendencies
cannot accept

i weep
for this knowledge
that is much too painful
and far too relevant
to be the only solution

Savior Jesus

Jesus
Compassionate Jesus
You said that You came to heal
You are my Healer
You are my Doctor
You are my Great Physician
So I am asking You tonight
To heal the parts of me
That are still broken
To wash over me with Your life
Until there is no trace of death
No stain
Nothing partial
But a wholeness
That only You can bring

Jesus
Awesome Jesus
You said that You came to set the captives free
You are my Champion
You are my Deliverer
You are my Defender
So I am asking You tonight
To deliver me from the things
That still bind me
To free me from the parts of my old self
That I have not been completely separated from
To protect me from my foes
That are too big for me
But never a match for You

Jesus
Perfect Jesus
You said that You are the Truth
You are my Way

You are the Lamp lighting my feet
You are the Light on my path
So I am asking You tonight
To come with Your truth
And apply it to the lies
That still live in me
The false things that still look me in the face
And stare me down
When I take my eyes off of You
Oh, great God
My Creator
My Source
My Author
My Sustainer
Come with Your light
And illuminate my path

Jesus
Living Jesus
You said that You came to show me
The way to life
You said that I would have to
Lay down my life
And pick up my cross
You said that the way would be narrow
You said that only a few would find it
So I am asking You tonight
To take my hand
And help me find my way
I am telling You tonight
That I want to keep you beside me
Always
That I never want to wander
I want to be a sheep who knows my Shepherd
I want to know Your voice
I want to know it well
So speak to me

For I am listening

Jesus
Savior Jesus
Every day
You bring me to life
And resurrect me again
Jesus
Savior Jesus
I am praising You tonight
That every morning
You make me brand new
And every moment
You are saving me

The Boy

The boy
has been
running
laps on the track
all day long.
The boy is bored;
(not tired, just bored.)

Now he wants to
take off his shoes
and run barefoot
along the gravel road,
alone,
into the night.

He says he will feel no pain.
He says he will be
back in the morning.
But I know
there will be
drops of blood
in his footprints;
and there will be
no returning…

Rebellion
(Satan Says)

It began for me
the way it always does

with a single thought
of either:

I can…
or *I don't have to…*

I can be better than You;
I don't have to listen to You.

It was the same thought
that overtook Eve,
the fruit in hand;

The same knocking
that came crouching
at Cain's door,
his brother's blood
already soaking up the ground.

The same filthy independence
that led Abraham into
Hagar's tent because

he couldn't wait.

I waited centuries for this
desert, to try you three times.

I'm still trying.

Beauty

Beauty ruins you
you see
because it sets a standard
raises the bar
to a place you can
never reach again
It opens up spaces
that will press you
with hunger
and refuse to be
satiated
A sieve
A bottomless ocean

Beauty makes you poor
you see
because it reminds you that
nothing belongs to you
none of it is yours
not even the skin you wear
so tight
or the eyes you dress up
so pretty

Beauty is consequence
you see
because it opens
your eyes
and makes them take in
first the light

and then the darkness that follows
never giving you a choice
or a say in the matter

It won't let those eyes close
Won't let that space fill
Won't let those hands reach
as high again

Beauty is sometimes
in the end
a painting washed over
black
on your biggest wall
without a frame

It is a one eyed monster
staring down at you
from the top of the telephone pole

What I Need Most

this humility
it's good for me
it presses me so low
that i have nowhere else to go
but back to the beginning
a humble and necessary beginning
an oak tree contained in a cruel shell

this brokenness
it heals me
in ways that
all the doctors
and psychics
and fortune tellers
and therapies
and theologies
and volumes of answers
never could
this brokenness
breaking down my face
in beautiful torrents
is what i need most

this cloud
with its irony
is what i lament under
while i wait for
some light, some good
some pieces for the whole
some wisdom, some fruit;

this can't be for nothing

i can't believe
that this is for nothing

Scared

Resistance.
Why this resistance?
No one is forcing me to be here;
I came of my own free will
And no one said I have to stay.
Yet after all this time
And all these faces
A year and a half later
The accuser's voice
Still rings in my ears—
Mocking.
Taunting.
And even when I try to shut it out
I still find myself feeling
Cowardly.
Scared to death.
Scared that I won't make it
That I am not good enough
That I don't have what it takes
To be what they want me to be
What they say I am.
Scared that my loins
Will never know anything but
Disgrace
Shameful passion
Forbidden pleasures.
Scared that my seed will never fall
On good soil
In a place where it can
Grow

And become something
With a face
And a name
A son
Or a daughter.
One of my very own
To know me
To look up to me
To love me.
I'm scared that
I will never hear them call me
Daddy
I'm afraid that all this pain
And toil
Could possibly be
A waste.
I shudder
And I cover my mouth
To think that this road
Might lead me to another
Dead end.
That this fairy tale
Might not have a happy ending.
I'm scared
But still
I have this little piece of hope
To hold onto.
This hope is named
Grace
And it is all I have left
To satisfy my hunger
And fill my empty belly

On the darkest night
When I am wide awake
Longing for the dawn
Aching for the first rays of morning
To creep past my window
Onto my face
And into my eyes
Drying my tears
And giving me strength
To get up and try
One more time
To get up and live
One more day.
Hoping
For something I cannot see.
Believing
In something bigger than me
Myself
And my silly fears.
Knowing
That I am precious
I am a prince
That I was made for
Something so much greater than this.
That I was crafted to occupy
A space much nobler
Than this rotting skin,
This flesh that so easily betrays me.
Maybe that's what I am
The most scared of
After all.

One Day With You

You know, Jesus
This time with You
These precious moments
In Your Word
In Your presence
They are the bread for my day
They are the water for my soul
When I am thirsty
When I am dry
I come and dip into these waters
I come and stoop low at Your fountain
And let You refresh me
Let You fill me
And I just have to say
Again
That I need this water
This Living water
This water that is alive and moving
Flowing
Refreshing
Reviving

You say
"All who are thirsty"
You beckon
"Come to the well"
You say
"You who have no money"
You tell me
"There will be no cost"
You offer an invitation
"Drink and never thirst again"
And it is to this invitation
That I respond gratefully
It is to this call that I come running

Panting
Longing
With my mouth
And my soul
And my spirit
Wide open for You
Ready to receive You
Because I have tasted
And I know
That You satisfy
Like nothing else can
I know that
One day with You
Is better than
A thousand anywhere else

Jesus

You are the crack of light

in my black hole

You are the whisper of hope

in my raging storm

Sunday Morning

pain.
those deep holes
no one can fill
but that you are always trying to fill
with all the things
that just keep leaking out
and leaving them
just as empty again.

desperation.
that place you go to
when you're all by yourself;
a place no one else can go with you
where your past
and sin
and the world
and life
have you backed into a corner
and give you the choice to either
throw up your hands and say
"i need you God"
or keep trying to climb the walls
that are only getting higher around you.

humility
is that place you get to
when you finally agree to be honest
with yourself and with God
about everything.
that place of brokenness
where you stop striving
stop trying
stop fighting
and just lay down on your face
and wait for the exchange:

everything you can't let go of
for something you could never earn

faith.
it turns on lights
that the darkness can't hide
and opens doors
that reason
and common sense
could never keep shut.

grace.
it finds you right where you are,
right there in your mess.
you don't have to go looking for it
but just sit and wait for it.
wait for it to say
"you can come out now;
you can stop hiding."
grace gives you the permission
to hold up the mess you have made
and know that it is a beautiful thing.
it is a beautiful mess
because now it is framed in mercy.
so now you can display it proudly
on your wall
and tell everyone about it.
nothing to be ashamed of
but only gratitude
that grace could make
something so beautiful
out of something so broken.

hope.
it is something you get
when you stop looking in
and start looking up.

it is something that makes you laugh
and say to yourself:

"i have been asking
all the wrong questions."
it is a voice that speaks
to the chaos
and confusion
and offers a new perspective.
it is a bold proclamation of:

"yes i am dirty
yes i am lost
yes i do need help;
but that's alright
because the solution was already there
waiting for me
long before i had the problem.
the search crew was already
prepared to come and find me
before i ever ran away."

hope is the hand
that helps you find your way home
and leads you to the table,
to the best seat in sight
and tells you to sit there
and feast on
what has been offered to you
freely.

Reasons

There are reasons why people do the things they do.

There are reasons why people will 'settle' for something that seems so absurd to others, but can be the exact thing that they need the most at that moment.

There are reasons why we go to great lengths to get one little thing, if that one thing promises a form of hope or salvation for us, even if no one else can see it.

There are reasons why some people forsake the ones closest to them and give up so much for what appears to be so little, if that little thing is everything to them.

There are reasons why people willingly suffer abuse, humiliation, and risk harm and fatalities for a form of attention or connection that they fear they might die without.

There are reasons why I fill myself with things that seem to fill me when I am empty even though they empty me more in the long run, because I can't stand to be empty for more than a moment, and can't bear the thought of being alone, ever.

There are reasons why Eve took the fruit in her hand and ate it—

and there are reasons why I am where I am now.

Careful

Just a piece of clay,
running away
from the potter

Just a little boy,
running away
from his father

Sometimes

I asked you
how can you

ever see
the light

when you live
your life

under a rock
and you said

the sun shines
down here too

sometimes

All the Others

Perhaps you were made to live
in this perpetual state of longing
so you could be the one

to ask the questions
that everyone else is wondering,

to speak the words that
everyone around you is thinking,

and to paint the pictures
that all the others are dreaming.

Coming to Repentance

The soul is such a fragile and peculiar thing—
the way it can resist the advances of a thousand daggers,
and then bleed to death at the solitary prick of a pin
—the way it can stand strong against the currents
of many rushing rivers and tumultuous waves,
only to drown in a single splash.
How is it that a person can sit cold-hearted
and dry-eyed for hours, listening to sobering speeches
and remain unaffected—but then sometimes all it takes
is one word to bring that person to their breaking point,
to unlock their soul and the flood of tears
that always comes with heartfelt emotion.

Sin is such a deceiving thing—
the way it appeals to you in your weakest moment,
promising satisfaction, fulfillment, and everything you've ever dreamed of
And then what does sin do, but leave you with a broken heart,
a full conscience and a lot of explaining to do.
No, sin has nothing good to offer
Sin is deadly, fatal, and evil—
if only more people could realize that from the outset,
before they give in to it and find themselves wrapped in its deadly coils.

Repentance is such a compelling thing—
the very idea that in a single moment of decision
a person can turn completely around and choose to take steps
in the opposite direction of where they were previously headed,
pledging to press on steadily and never look back—
that a person can go from darkness to light all at once
And in that moment of repentance,
the very things that kept their hands clasped so tight for so long
can be let go of and forgotten;
and how glad the hands are at that moment to see those things go!

Forgiveness is such a far reaching thing
I love the way it can change everything in an instant,
overlooking wrongs and accepting apologies that have not even yet surfaced
There you stand, guilty with a tearstained face,
and what does forgiveness do?
It comes to you with a shoulder,
a resting place for your head and tears,
and with arms of love and acceptance to wrap around you,
telling you not to feel bad about anything
It loves you immensely, even though you know through and through
that you don't deserve anything good, certainly not love,
surely not love of this magnitude, not after everything you've done.

Love is such an amazing thing
So steadfast, so constant, so consummately wonderful!
Love is there at the beginning of the journey
with a careful shove and a smile, and it is there at the end as well,
with tears and an embrace
Love exists just as strongly and assuredly
when you can't feel it or even find a trace of it
as it does when you feel your heart bursting with vibrancy and fulfillment,
and are consumed completely by love's complexity.

Love is always there,
even when you foolishly choose to leave it
and wander on your own for awhile and then return
The heart can take comfort in the fact that love will never give up
You know it will always be there,
because love cannot leave, it cannot turn back,
and it could never deny another,
because do so would mean denying itself .

Salvation

There are days I look so long and hard
At what is not
That I fail to see all that is

Who is it that gives me permission to stare at a wall
And see upon it nothing at all?

Who is it that told me a hole is a hole
And not a big, beautiful empty space about to be filled?

Who is it that convinced me not to see hope but despair?

There is a new pair of eyes
My salvation is peering through them

There is a humble place
My salvation will come from there

glad

be glad
for the pain
that cuts you deep,
for it is forging a river
to flow and heal
children not yet created,
faces not yet named or known,
a current rising to form
new oceans to be sailed upon

be glad
for the spaces in you
yet to be filled,
for they are inviting a chorus
so rich and pure
and strong
that even angels
will envy its voice
and wish they had thought
to compose such a sound

The Way You Speak About Your Children

makes me believe that God must
still have room in his heart for me.

A Very Good Thing

Sometimes
when things get all cloudy
and chaotic,
every once in awhile,
you just have to let go.

Take your hands off of it,
let it float away from you
out of your reach completely
in widening squares and circles.

It's not that you're giving up;
it's that you're finally seeing things
as they actually are.

It's that you're coming
from fantasy to reality,
leaving the sand and muck
to find your footing on some stone,
knowing that you can't get it back—

(You don't want it back.)
And you can't ever get it back.

And that's a very good thing
for someone like you.

From the North to the South

There is a lighthouse
Shining its light for me
Standing tall and proud
Lighting my path so I can see

There is a voice
Echoing over the waves
Makings its way to my listening ears
Urging assurance to stay

There is a warm peace
Floating over the waters
Calming this raging sea
Flowing straight from the Father

Oh, how I need to see your light
For without it my feet can only stumble
as I wander through this dark night

Oh, how I need to hear your voice
For without it my direction wavers,
and there is nothing to determine my every choice

Oh, how I need to feel your peace
For without it my heart can only race,
and worries never cease

There is a gentle breeze
Blowing from the north to the south
Driving me to my knees
Putting thankfulness in my mouth

All These Things

All these things I do
I know I must do for a reason
All the crazy, random, stupid, impulsive things
And all the selfless, beautiful, worthwhile, meaningful things I do.
I guess I do these various things
Because I know no other way
I know no other life
Other than this one I am living, day after day
And so I will continue to do all these things
Until I resolve to change;
To turn my face and choose another way

All these things I feel
I know I must feel because of my past,
and the pain I carry inside
Entertaining impressions take precedence
over honest depictions of the truth,
because so often I feel like
I have no one in whom I can confide
So who I really am, and feel I ought to be
Gets buried under and drowned out by
All the things I wish I could be,
And the person I hope to someday become
And so by forgetting who I really am
At this present moment,
I find myself getting no closer to the me
I always hoped to be;
And in doing so, by living in constant denial,
I am doing myself no justice
All these things I say
The words I form and articulate
To paint a picture for the world to see,
A definition of who I want them
To believe I really am, mean nothing
I speak the truth

I tell many lies
I long to live
And sometimes I wish I could just die
Because it seems like all I do is try and try
To build a reputation for myself,
And prove to the world that
I am real and the words I say are true;
When I don't even have a clue
Who I am myself
All these things I believe and know
They consume me with fear,
Crippling me until
I know not which way to go

All these things I see and hear
And learn from the world I live in
And occupy with my very breath,
They burn holes in me
like little sparks from a raging fire
A fire that won't stop burning
Until it has succeeded at consuming
Every part of me,
Leaving me with no trace of hope
No promise of a better tomorrow—
Only charred dreams and blackened emotions
Forgotten in a worthless heap on the ground

All these things I have claimed as my own
The stature I have acquired as I have grown
The friends I have made,
the songs I have sung,
The players I have played,
and the ones I have truly loved;
they leave me feeling empty and bitter
My regrets leave me cold and shallow
I have no hope for tomorrow
Unless I let myself be stripped bare

And purged to my very marrow;
Until I allow You to flood my thoughts and my mind,
Redirecting my every intention
and redefining who I am as a person;
a creation, an individual, a gift to mankind;
reclaiming all the life that has been drained out of me;
until I realize that only You can truly satisfy,
that only You hold the keys to everything that matters,
Until I am found to be a pure, spotless,
Innocent Child of God,
Resting safely in your loving hands
With no failures, no faults,
No accomplishments and no rewards
Until I stop investing in the things of this world
And fix my eyes on eternity,
Then and only then
Will all these things
Start to make sense to me.

Eternity in My Hands

i have experienced religion without God
church without Jesus
christianity without the Spirit
and it is as empty as a well
that used to hold water
but can't remember how
or when
it finally ran dry

it is as dry and tasteless
as a cardboard box
a splintered crate
having served its purpose
waiting to be carried away

i have known the feeling
of waiting every day for something
that can only be furthered by my self
and my own faith
i have known and carried the burden
of moments and days wasted
on indecision and faithlessness

i have tried to suffocate and strangle a passion
that could never die
a flame that could never go out
because it is eternal—

it is eternity i hold in my hands
and in my heart
and that is a heavy, inescapable weight to carry

Full Circle

How do you forgive yourself
When you run out of excuses
When you have no more apologies
No more rationalizations
No more copouts
Only reasons
Why you are this way
Why you do the things you do

How do you explain something to someone
Who couldn't understand you
Even if they wanted to
How do you hold love in your hands
And believe for an instant
That it might do you some good
When all you've ever known of love
Is shame
Regret
Sorrow
And hurt
How do you get over something like that
And how do you ever forget

How do you sit and watch the world
When it has become your prison
And you its only captive
Its sole victim
How do you keep on fighting
When it's you against the world
Every day, every time

When every battle is lost
How do you find the strength
To keep on doing it
Over
And over
And over again

How do you rid the pain
When it's all you've ever known
How do you erase the guilt and the fear
When they have become
Your only companions
Your only excuse
Your only reason
To get out of bed every single day
And keep on running
Toward an endless disillusionment

How do you sit and watch the world
With a smile on your face
When all you want to do is scream
Let out all your bitterness
Your resentment
Your anger and your rage
How can anything in life look beautiful through your eyes
These new eyes that you wear

How do you deal with the insanity
Every single day
How can you live with yourself
And continue on in this way
How long can such a thing go on

Until you reach the end of yourself
And find that you are
Back at the very beginning again,
Just getting started

Metaphor

I am Adam
The fruit already on my lips
I have tasted and now
My eyes are open

I am Abraham
Leaving the familiar
Walking on in obedience
My faith firmly grounded

I am Joseph
Resisting temptation
You never give me more
Than I can bear

I am Moses
Eternity on my mind
Giving up momentary pleasures
For your ultimate glory

I am Joshua
Strong and courageous
Leading the weary
To sweet victory

Tug of War

How easily my spiritual house crumbles
One brick out of place
The entire foundation lies in disgrace

I let the Enemy into your house
Sit down next to him on the couch
And put my arm around him

Until I find your eyes
A gaze of grace
To disable the lies

I am such a wretched sinner
But in your book
Still a winner

Because Jesus died for me
Lost his breath
To set me free

Now I know the price of love
Giving every part of yourself
You said that would be enough

And so I learn to walk by faith
One foot after the other
A little closer every day

Knowing I am already free
And all you ask
Is that I claim the victory

Life Eternal

I wait on You today, oh Lord— and no sooner do I turn my ear toward You than I hear Your voice speaking to me, telling me what it is you require of me, what it is that pleases You, what it is you want me to do next.

I look at this field and see that it is still rough in places. Looking closely, I can tell that there are certain portions that are still unplowed.

I look at this gold in my hand and am disgusted to find these impurities still staring back at me. I am ashamed to find not a pure reflection of You, but still more of myself.

And so I see the ever present need for Your hand, and yet I do not despair. I do not drown in hopelessness, because I know that You, my God, are faithful to finish what You start. You are careful to bring to completion all the things that You give birth to and set into motion.

My flesh cringes, struggles under Your hand, even dares to throw a tantrum, like a foolish and unwilling child— but my spirit leaks wisdom and spills some light on my soul— and for this I am grateful.

For this wisdom I gladly submit myself yet again to your plow. For this truth You have unleashed in me I willingly step back into the hottest part of the fire, to the very middle where the intensity reddens and puts to ash everything that is not of value, leaving only the pure and useful things that were made for this purpose and this purpose only— to reflect Your glory.

I am humbled to find that I am still very much human. There is still much work to be done. Even after these weeks of refining, the flesh in me still puts up a good fight against Your every move.

But I rejoice to see how You have begun to change me already. To see how my will has been gradually subjected, submitting not all at once, but gradually, one little ounce at a time, to the entire weight of Your desire for me, to the fullness of Your will that makes no provision for my flesh and leaves no room for my own will and desire.

I am glad to see that I am a little quicker to obey now— that my flesh gives up a little sooner and submits a little more willingly to Your conviction. And when I do fall down, I am much quicker to get back up now than before. I am much quicker to respond to You, to turn back to You, because I know that life is only found in You, and that to stay in the dark is like death to me— death that only rots my soul and tortures me from the inside out.

I praise You, Father, that with You there is hope. I praise You that You are such a patient Father, so willing to take us by the hand and lead us away from harm, away from our own foolishness, into a spacious place of rest and abundance, a place where we can drink from You and begin to find that we don't have to thirst all the time anymore— that we don't have to strive or grasp or beg— but simply receive what You are offering us freely— a full life. Abundant life. Life in Your Spirit. Life that is eternal and starts right now.

Humility

Unforgiveness is a prison that no one else can possibly get me out of. They can beckon to me from the outside, they can point out for me the key that lies at my feet, they can advise me to reach down and take hold of it, but I— I must be the one to reach down and pick up the key and unlock the door.

This key is made of humility, and I have found humility to be a substance that possesses both the qualities of being as light as a feather and yet as heavy as a stone at the same time.

It is a thing with such a weight that I must crouch down painfully low to even lift it off the ground; but once I take it in my arms and rise to my feet, it becomes as light and free as a single feather, so light that I feel like I could carry it around with me forever and never put it back down again.

The Best Thing

The best thing I can do
Is be honest
with myself
with others
with the God of my soul
with my Creator, my Other

The best thing I can do
Is quit pretending to be someone
or something
that I am not
and start living
like someone who knows what they want
Someone who has charted out their course
a traveler whose journey is set
a warrior whose goal is decided
Like a child who has known fear
but who is not afraid of anything—
neither what creeps up from behind
or what runs on ahead,
because he knows what it means
to go beyond and rise above:
to overcome

The best thing I can do
Is simply quit trying so hard
just stop fighting
let my hands fall limp at my sides
Surrender
and sit still for long enough
to hear the sweet things
that are filling my ears,
and let them settle there,
like lions in their den,
like birds in their nest

When I Look At Your Love

I look up at the stars
And I am amazed
I know you created every one of them

I look at all my sins
And I am ashamed
I know that you have forgiven every one of them

I look at my past
And I am confused
I know that you have been with me all along

I look at my life
And I am hopeful
I know you have plans for me

I look at your truth
And I am inspired
I know your truth is setting me free

I look at your grace
And I am humbled
I know you want to use me for your glory

I look at your love
And I am unworthy
I know you loved me then and you are loving me now

Abiding

Lies, lies, stop these lies!
I am addicted to them
I can't stop telling them
And hurting everyone I know
And everyone I love
By my deception
My continual hypocrisy
If an honest tongue is what you desire, God
If a repentant heart is fertile ground
Then come sow your seeds of truth in me
Bring your plow to turn up this soil
Infested with disgusting lies

Sin, sin, take away my sin!
I am bound to it
I am defined by it
My very reputation,
My face and my name
Are known for it
All this worldliness
This selfishness
These disgusting habits
And destructive behavior
That I hate
And I love
Every moment of every day
As my flesh fights
In an intense spiritual war
As the forces of good and evil
Battle for my soul

Pride, foolish pride, release me!
Open your grip and let me fall
Out of your reach
Let me humble myself

And grovel at the feet of a holy God
Let my heart be broken
Smashed to pieces
And put back together again
The way it was supposed to be
The way God intended
So that I can live a life of holiness
Before my awesome God
So that I don't have to dishonor His name
Time and time again
By my self-centered actions
By these foolish intentions
That run me ragged
And give me reason to think
That I have a right to live this way
That I don't have to answer to anyone

Life, sweet breath of life, let me breathe!
Open up my lungs and grant me air
So that I can exhale
So that I can live
In freedom
Shamelessly
With meaning and purpose
With solemn direction
As a child who knows his father well
And listens to His voice,
Obeying His commands,
And walking down the road
That was appointed to him
Long before he got off track
And wandered into forbidden fields
Tasting things that were not meant for him
Learning things he was never supposed to know

Love, everlasting love, save my soul!
How I long to be made new

To be complete and whole
To find a place where I can stop
And rest in peace
No more grasping
No more searching
No more longing
But simply abiding
In your truth
Your precious promises
Your mercies
That are new every time I wake

It Takes Some Faith

It takes more than just a little time
To change something
When you are so used to things
Just the way they are
When you can't imagine your life
Any other way

It takes more than a day
To change yourself
When you decide that you are not happy
With the person you have become
When you want to start doing things differently
You want to walk away
But a small part of you wants to stay
Right where you are

It takes some faith sometimes
To believe in something real
Something you cannot see
But only believe in,
Because you have hope
That there is something better out there
A life of meaning
An ocean of peace for you to dive into
When you reach its banks someday

It takes some perseverance
To get where you want to go
The second step is painful
Unlike the first
Taken out of reckless abandon

The first step was by far the easiest
It is easy to keep promises to yourself for a day
But then you wake up the next day

And you have to decide for yourself
If you are strong enough
If you believe enough in yourself
And in your God
To follow through

So you make it another minute, another hour, another day;
That's progress
So you go to sleep and wake up to yet another day
Another time for decision
Will I remain true to myself and my commitment
Or will my faith falter when things get harder
When I feel myself being forced outside my comfort zone
When the truth starts to chip at these walls
That have become my security,
My comfort

Will I be strong enough to say
Let the walls fall down
Am I willing to let my very identity be crushed to dust
In my search for the ultimate truth

What Does It Mean

What does it mean
To walk by faith
Trusting you to guide me
Every step of the way
What does it mean
And how will I know
If I am walking by faith
And not by sight

What does it mean
To be in the world
But not of it
To be associated with something
But not defined by it
What does it mean
And how will I know
If my heart is in
The right place

What does it mean
To truly surrender
Sacrificing
Letting go
Giving up something of mine
For something better
Something that can only come from You
What does it mean
And how will I know
If I am really letting go

What does it mean
To be renewed
To be emptied of the old
And replace it with something new
Something more fulfilling

Something to satisfy
Something to quench my thirst
For more than a day
What does it mean
And how will I know
If I am a new creation

What does it mean
To really love God
Making my every move
An act of praise
Seeking to know Him more
Each and every day
Believing that He knows best
Resting in His promises
What does it mean
And how will I know
If I really love God

Saved

You don’t mind the
waywardness in me

because you remember
Eden and you know

evil is just misplaced
desire born out of

a need these bodies
can’t fill—

You don’t mind
the chaff in my eyes

because you know
that behind them

there is a fire burning
pure and strong

a fire that you stoke
night and day with

the pulse of your
great faith

a fire that will
not stop burning

until all that remains
is the faith itself

a faith that will save
me from myself

oh how I need to be
saved from myself

Battling With Pride

You say you want to change
You tell me this is not the life you want to live
But day after day you continue on in this way
Night after night I watch you drifting farther away…

And so, because I am your friend,
And because I care for you so deeply,
I must ask you:
Do you really want to change?
Do you seek to know the ultimate truth?
This past that you speak so regretfully of;
Are you ready now to let go of it;
To say honestly, "I surrender…
I give it up; I want no part of it.
The past shall have no hold on me."

For you cannot move on until you let go
You cannot be healed until you have acknowledged your wound.
You cannot be filled with new and better things
until you have been emptied of the old and the useless.

I dare to say that you are letting your pride get in the way
of everything you want, and everything you need.
Sometimes healing begins with something as simple
as an apology without an excuse.
Maybe you need to reevaluate your reasons for holding on
And ask yourself, "Is this really what I want?
Is this the life I will choose for myself?"

Someday your desire for change will be so much greater than your present desire to always be right and always look your best in front of everyone.
Maybe then you will come to the point of abandonment that will release your pain and applaud your humility and free your soul.

Maybe on that day you will humble yourself to the point of saying,
"I was wrong. I am unworthy.
I am not good enough.
I need help."

Help and advice are there in abundance
And they can be yours;
All you must do is ask for them, and you will receive.
Only you can know the joy that can be yours,
The joy that is found is finding yourself.
The peace that erases all doubts and fills every void;
It can only be born after pride is destroyed.

Break Me

Fill me, God
Fill me with your life
Your life everlasting

Guide me, God
Guide me down your paths
Your paths of righteousness

Teach me, God
Teach me of your plans
The plans you have been saving for me

Show me, God
Show me what to do
What I can do to honor You

Save me, God
Save me from this sin
This sin that has encompassed me

Protect me, God
Protect me from this world
This world that has no knowledge of You

Break me, God
Break this heart
This heart that was made to praise you

Somewhere Inside Me

Somewhere inside me
Are spaces waiting to be filled
A home I long to find
A house I hope to build

Somewhere inside me
Are questions seeking answers
A thoughtful string of melodies
A patient row of dancers

Somewhere inside me
Are all the things I feel
A restless misdirection
A search for something real

Somewhere inside me
Is a breath of inspiration
The hope of a better future
A sweet promise of restoration

Somewhere inside me
It's your voice I hear
Asking me to wait
Telling me not to fear

Somewhere inside me
I hear you whisper my name
Reminding me of your forgiveness
Telling me you love me just the same

Somewhere inside me
Is a peace that can't be explained
Truth that won't be denied
Joy that can't be contained

Somewhere inside me
Chains are falling to the ground
You are taking my heart captive
I was lost but now I'm found

Somewhere inside me
Is faith as small as a mustard seed
Believing that You are the only one
Who can give me all that I need

Somewhere inside me
There is truth to combat all the lies
That threaten to destroy me
And plot my soul's demise

Somewhere inside me
I know that there is a reason
For every road I have walked down
For each and every season

Somewhere inside me
Are all the spaces that once seemed so small
This little boy inside me never dreamed
That he could stand so tall

Somewhere inside me
Is a godly man
Underneath all that I do
And everything I am

Somewhere inside me
Is sincerity
An earnest will to fight
A desire to do what is right

Somewhere inside me
I believe that you are my God
I don't know who you are
But I believe that you are my God

Found A Place

I am tired of crying these tears
Ashamed of so many wasted years
Filled with nothing but regrets and fears

I am throwing away this pain
I will stand with hands lifted in the pouring rain
Joy is filling up my heart; I simply cannot refrain

I am done with living this life of lies
The deeper I sink, the louder my heart cries
I may have missed the show,
but I am returning for the triumphant reprise

I refuse to continue in this depressed state of mind
Meaning I will seek, and purpose I will find
I am leaving this world of confusion behind

I will stand proudly when they play my song
I will admit that I have been wrong
I have finally found a place where I belong

I'm Ready

I'm ready to let go of it
To learn to rise above it
And say, "What of it?"

I'm ready to hear your voice
I'm making this my choice
Watch the souls rejoice

I'm ready now to arrive
At this place for which we all strive
It makes us come alive

I'm ready to take your hand
And run to distant lands
Please make me understand

I want to know your truth
I want to believe in you
I'm ready to be made brand new

How Many Times

How many books stand half-read on the shelf
How many good intentions are stacked there as well
Buried dreams
Discarded hopes
Out come the seams
Unraveled thread on the rope

How many times have I vowed 'never again'
How many promises have I made, and then
There I go
Foolishly
Throwing away the plans
That you formed for me

How many lessons will I learn
How long will this fire continue to burn
Until I cry
In humility
Here am I
Take all of me

Hibernation

there is mourning after the loss
a time for the spirit to be broken and shed its tears
there is pain in realizing the cost
in seeing the price you have paid down through the years

the old has gone but the new has not yet come
shattered souls long to feel safe and sound
the flower is bitter at the scorching sun
but the seed falls thankfully to the ground

bathe yourself in turmoil and sorrow
but perseverance says there is something to be gained
who's to say when you wake up tomorrow
that any of these feelings will still remain

Alas

Alas, I have found my voice
How freeing it is to be able to say in confidence:
"I have made my choice."

Alas, my heart is finally set
On moving forward, on finding a better life:
on learning to forget.

Alas, I am spreading my wings
In time I will soar with grace and strength:
And how my heart will sing!

Alas, I now know the reason
Of love and laughter, of joy and regret:
I am breathing deep. I am finding my reason.

And no one can take that from me.

Divinity

I am broken, I am empty
You are healing, you are full

I am ugly, I am dirty
You are beautiful, you are pure

I am deceit, I am lies
You are perfect, you are truth

I am fearful, I am running
You are patient, you are calling

I am anger, I am desperation
You are peace, you are salvation

I am lonely, I am worthless
You are comfort, you are value

I am separation, I am distance
You are restoration, you are unity

I am selfish, I am pride
You are giving, you are humility

I am measured, I am confined
You are eternal, you are boundless

I am human, I am man
You are God, you are divine

I am loved, I am yours
You are forgiving, you are mine

You Will Find Me

When you close your eyes and breathe a silent prayer
I will not be far;
You will find me there

My ears are always open and listening,
whenever you call out to me
My arms are always open,
waiting for you to fall into them
Whether you are obeying me or running away from me
I am your God;
I created you
I will never stop pursuing you,
and my love for you will never end

When your heart skips a beat
at the sight of my magnificent creation
When you see a breathtaking display of my beauty
In a moment of truth, a moment of salvation
When your heart's in the right place,
That's when you will find me

You will find me in the quiet moments of peace
And in the gentle times of rest
You will find me in the midst of a stormy sea
And at the end of the road, after you have stood the test

In the faces of your children
In the eyes of your enemy
In the Words I have spoken to you
These are the places you will find me

I am a God who wants to be found
If only my people would open their eyes
and look around
In a church, on the street, far from home, across the sea

I am waiting;
Won't you come and find me

I told you I loved you
And to prove my love, I came to you
I entered your world and paid the greatest price
Because I loved you
You say you love me
Then why don't you come to me too
Come and enter into the wonderful life
that I have prepared for you
I died for you;
I only ask you to live for me
I will lead the way;
You have only to walk behind me

When you seek me with all your heart
That, my child, is when you will find me

Love Will

When acquaintances doubt and friends wonder,
love will believe

Acquaintances assume, friends question,
love trusts

When an acquaintance falls and a friend wavers,
love will stand

Acquaintances rarely do, friends usually do,
love always does

When an acquaintance gives up and a friend grows weary,
love will persevere

When all acquaintances have rusted
and all friendships have grown dusty,
love shines through

Acquaintances forget, friends faintly recall,
love remembers

While acquaintances fear and friends worry,
love calms

When acquaintances talk and friends whisper,
love is silent

When acquaintances are impatient and friends want to see results,
love waits

When acquaintances are oblivious
and friends are catching glimpses,
love sees clearly

Acquaintances usually let you down,
friends can sometimes be trusted,
love can be counted on

Acquaintances are built on common interests,
friendships are built on common goals and desires,
love is built on a common creed

Acquaintances last for a season, friends last a lifetime,
love lasts an eternity

When acquaintances won't and friends might—

love will

You Tell Me

I tell you that I am tired
And you tell me to get behind the wheel,
turn the key, and start driving
I ask you where we are going
And you tell me it matters not where we are going
But that you are going with me

I tell you the journey is too long,
That this feat is impossible,
That everything seems hopeless
And you tell me that faith has nothing to do with common sense,
That real faith will lead me far beyond
The realms of human reasoning and human understanding

I tell you that I am weak
And you tell me that you will give me the strength
To get to where I need to be

I utter fragments of my pain and confusion
And you speak truth back to me
I spill out my unending questions
And you meet my doubts with answers

I tell you that I want to be complete, that I long to be whole
And you tell me that I will indeed have abundant life
As I learn to trust you, as I begin to walk down your path
And cling tightly to your truth

I tell you that I want everything to make sense right now, today,
That I don't think I can hold out any longer
And you tell me that in time my faith will be rewarded
But that first it must be tested
And put through the flames and deep waters
That I must first be completely broken and emptied
Before I can be restored

Before life is breathed back into my bones
And peace is flowing through my soul
With currents deep enough to cover the past
Strong enough to wash away this confusion
Pure enough to erase every sin

I tell you that I am willing to wait,
That I will choose to trust you
Even when things seem impossible
And the future looks grim and uninviting;
And you tell me that you will be with me always,
That I will never have to face the giants
Without you by my side

I hang my head and say, I'm sorry, Father
For disappointing you so many times…
For wandering so far away from you
That I couldn't even hear you calling out my name

You lift my tear stained eyes to meet yours,
And you tell me:
You are completely forgiven and eternally loved
I ask you how you can possibly look on me
When I am so saturated in my so many sins;
Such selfishness; such pride
And you tell me, *My precious son,*
It is for these very things that I died

I Am

I am a creek bed
Thirsty and dry
Flood me with your rivers
Rain down on me from the sky

I am a canvas
Anxiously waiting
To see the parts of me
That you are still creating

I am a vessel
At rest in the harbor
Awaiting the command
Of the wind's gentle lure

I am a candle
A wick and some wax
Burning myself with passion
Never looking back

I am a face, a name
An idea, a dream
I am everything and nothing
I am more than I seem

Every Day

Every day
It is the same old story
I get up, I shower, I dress
I go to work
I cheat, I lie, I swear
I try to get ahead
And do my best to look good in front of everyone
I complain about my sore back and my tired feet
I come home, eat dinner
And go to bed
It is the same old thing
Every day
The same old schedule
The same faces
The same roads
The same sights and sounds and smells
Haunting reminders of what my life has become
It is the same old nonsense
The same meaningless shuffle
Every day

Every day
You are loving me
Every moment of every day
You are pursuing me, chasing after me, calling out my name
When I take the time to stop and listen
You offer me little reminders
That you have never stopped loving me
Never stopped desiring and planning the very best for me
You offer me joy and peace in abundance,
And when I am humble enough,
Honest enough to admit that you know better than I do,
I reach out and take hold of these things
You teach me, and when I am still enough
To listen and hear your voice,

I learn just a little more of you and your ways
Every day

Every day
Life is a struggle
Every day
Temptation calls out my name
Trying to lure me back into the darkness
Telling me that I would be much happier
If I would only give in and go back to living in sin,
In worldliness, in freedom

Every day
I get on my knees before your throne
Every day
I ask you for strength
To take the next step
When I fall flat on my foolish face
I get up on feeble legs
And beg you for forgiveness

Every day
I am more and more amazed at your undying love
And your unalterable faithfulness to me
Every day
I long less and less for the things of this world
Every day
I find myself wanting just a little bit more of you God
Every day
My desires are changing
And as my desires change I find my actions changing too

Every day
I feel my faith growing
Just a little bit stronger
Every day
I look more and more like a child of God

As I begin to reflect your glory
And weave your ways into my steps, my words, my intentions

Every day
You remind me
That I have to keep trusting you
Every single day
And that this journey is a process
And I can only get there by placing one foot in front of the other
And taking one step at a time
As you guide me and show me where to go

Every day
You are with me
Every day
You love me just as much as the day before
Every day
I remember that you died for me
And I believe you would do it all over again
To see my life count for you
And make some kind of difference
Every day

submerged

my soul is
a sponge
and you are
the hand
that wrings
the drips
out of me
everything of this world
that i have
soaked up
you squeeze out
so you can
submerge me
in your holy fountain
drown me in your
purity
your holiness
your spring of
living water

dip me under
and don't let me
surface again
submerged in you
that's what i want
inside your presence
that's what i need
so take this world from me, jesus
take it all away
for you are the potter
and i am the clay
so come and have your way with me

Hourglass

Refuge, sweet refuge
With you I am safe
From all time and space

Freedom from self
Beckoning truth
Knowledge of wealth

Progress, forward movement
Step after fragile step
Eyes fixed on the end

Life, precious gift of life
Offered, granted
Disputed, recanted

Prison, coiled in thought
To know you, to find myself
To know my desires

Pain, self-inflicted, invited
Hypocrisy; earfuls of lies
A path of self demise

Hope, sweet promise of hope!
Blessings for tomorrow
A better life to follow

Never Stop Praising You

Psalm 103

I praise You God, my Father,
With all my soul
With everything that is within me
I praise Your holy Name

I will not forget Your abundant kindness to me
You are the one who
Forgives all my sins
And heals all my diseases

You deliver my life from the pit
You crown me with Your loyal love and compassion
You satisfy my life with good things
So that my youth is renewed like an eagle's

You do what is fair
You execute justice for me when I am oppressed
You are compassionate and merciful

You, oh Lord, demonstrate great loyal love
You do not always accuse
Or stay angry

You do not deal with me
As my sins deserve
You do not repay me
As my misdeeds deserve

For as high as the skies are above the earth
So Your loyal love towers over
Your faithful followers

As far as the eastern horizon is from the west

So You remove the guilt of my rebellious actions from me
As a Father has compassion on his children
So You have compassion on your faithful followers

For You know what we are made of
You realize we are made of clay
My life is like grass
Like a flower in a field it flourishes
But when the wind blows by, it disappears
And no one can even spot the place where it once grew

But because I am Your faithful follower
You, oh Lord, continually show Your loyal love to me
And You will do the same to all my descendants
To those who keep Your covenant
And carefully obey Your commands

You have established Your throne in Heaven
Your kingdom extends over everything
Even the angels praise You,
The powerful warriors who carry out your decrees
And obey Your orders
All Your servants who carry out your desires
Praise You as well

Everything that You have made
Is praising You in all the regions of Your kingdom
And my own soul will never stop praising You

Mercy

I looked down
at my broken bones
and then at the task
set before me,
and I asked God
what He was doing.

He answered:

"I'm teaching You
how to let my strength
be made perfect
in your weakness."

I looked down at the
light next to my feet
that was not growing
brighter, but actually
getting dimmer
with each step I took,
and I asked God
what He was doing.

He answered:

"I'm teaching you
how to trust me
more fully."

I looked up at the
mountains in front of me,
which were even bigger
and more intimidating
than the ones before,
and I asked God

what He was doing.

He answered:

"I'm teaching you
how to stretch your
faith in me."

I held out my hands
filled with all the things
that were becoming
too heavy for me to carry,
all the things I had
picked up along the way,
and I asked God
what He was doing.

He answered:

"I'm teaching you
how to throw yourself
on my mercy."

know

know that your house,
dimly lit and pressed there
against the world,
has within it a hallway
of many doors
that have not yet been opened;
that it holds countless rooms
for you which have not yet
been trodden upon

know that there is a room there
named Hope that has been
waiting for you since the day
that you were born

go to that room,
let it receive you,
and vow to stay there until
you see from the window
possibility instead of despair,
fullness, not a lack

stay there in that room
until the weight of all that
has pressed you builds and
constructs itself into a bridge,
a stage, a collection plate
ready to take up all that
you simply offer

know that others will
find you and join you there,
that you will not finish alone
but with a hand in yours,
a table set to nourish,

a fountain deep enough
to flow through your furthest
pain and most constant,
furious longing, an image
to mirror your own…

The Fearless Question

What is love?
Love is not happiness
Love is not easy
Love does not necessarily mean peace and joy
No, love is cruel; love is harsh
This I have learned, and stake my life by it:

To choose love is to choose pain
To choose grace is to choose suffering
To choose life over death
is to choose perseverance over instant gratification
To choose Your way over mine
is to give up what appears to be fulfilling
and pursue something that seems so unsatisfying,
knowing that actually the opposite is true

Love is not fun
Love does not taste good, and it is not easy to swallow
Love does not always promise healing and restoration
Love is not sunsets and ocean views and perfect unity

This is what love was meant to be
But love was broken; love was wounded
Sin entered the world, stifling love's flame
When sin took its birth, love received a new name

Now that the dust has cleared, those of us who choose love even still
see it in a much different light
And so we must ask ourselves the question that will shape our destinies,
and be the deciding factor for our souls:

Do we still want love?
Not the love we knew

But love, just as it is
The reality, the intensity, the coldness;
That is love

The world is watching
And God is waiting
Never ceasing to ask the fearless question
for the timid and the bold alike to stand and answer

Loving Discipline

How very much like the
cautious rainbow after
the storm daring to
sparkle more and more
vibrantly is the smile
on the Father's face
after he lovingly disciplines
one of His children.

How very much also
is the thunder like the
sound of His voice—
surprising and terrifying
at times, yet in its
resonance inviting a
pause and then reverence.

On Any Given Day

On any given day of my life
I am about a month's worth of discipline
away from where I want to be
spiritually, physically,
emotionally and relationally.

believe

we have to believe
in the years our days will compose
in the masterpiece
the grand tapestry
that is being woven by our moments
pressed down and held together
by our steps
our words
our recklessness
and greatest of intentions

we have to believe in these years
or we will see our lives
as only days to be lived
one at a time
without a purpose or a reason
for pressing on from this one to the next
without seeing the thread
that connects one to the others

we have to believe
in the days our years are composed of
when the future and the past
seem too far apart
we have to look and see
the steps that bridge the gap
between what was and what is to come
between who we are and who we will be
we have to believe in these days
and put stakes on their significance
or we might fail to see
the pieces and parts that make up the whole
the building blocks that make the building
to stand proud and strong
a structure with a solid foundation

a blueprint followed to a T

we have to believe in eternity
or we will miss the reasons why
we do what we do
from day to day
when we are stuck in time
and wonder if we will ever escape it
we have to remember
and know
that we were not made for it
we have to believe in the brevity of life
or we will hang on too tightly
and too long
to things that are fleeting
and passing away
out of our grip
out of sight
to things that will not last

we have to believe
in something greater than ourselves
or we will live as though the world was made
to serve and benefit and give to us
instead of the other way around

When You Begin

in the silence,
i can hear love's voice still speaking...

and he says to me:

when you begin to speak,
walls will come crumbling down around you

and when you begin to move,
mountains will move with you

when you begin to pray,
the young and the old will intercede
with grateful tears with you

when you begin to fight,
hosts of angels will war beside you

when you begin to break,
chains of every kind will break around you

when you begin to sing,
the trees and the oceans will burst forth in praise

when you begin to believe,
the dead will peek their heads from their rotting graves,
and bones will become flesh again

when you begin to love,
sinners and saints will pause from their labor to marvel

and when you truly begin to live,
all of creation will come alive with you

Love's Sting

When love is happening inside of me,
I can see it in my eyes
taste it in my breath
hear it in my words
and feel it in my footsteps;
because love cannot be contained.

Love, by its very nature,
cannot stay hidden or chained,
but must be let loose,
set free to ignite,
occupy, capture, impregnate,
and poison everything around itself
with its beautiful sting...

Exchange

I do not want to fill books with deep truths or speak words of great insight for people to sit and marvel at. I want to experience Your presence, and the power that comes with it. If people are impacted and changed by anything I say or do, I want it to be Your presence in me that changes them, and nothing else.

The power of Your presence that reaches out and grabs them in the place of their deepest need. Your truth convicting them in their deepest depravity. Your light piercing straight into the deepest darkness. I want it to be You in me that they see that changes them, that brings them from death to life, from darkness into Your marvelous light.

My greatest frustration is not in trying to get this power to dwell inside of me, but it is in knowing that this power is already there, that it has always been there since the moment I first believed.

Yet it is my own wretched skin, my own rotting, stinking flesh that hinders and corrupts and contains this life inside so that it is not always allowed to flow forth freely as it should, as you intend for it to.

My detriment lies in this body that I cannot separate myself from--but my hope lies in the glorious fact that this body is indeed already dead! What a joyous discovery this is— to find that I have been crucified with Christ, with my awesome Savior, and that it is not I that lives, but Christ in me.

This is my hope, the hope of glory— that I no longer live. This is in fact my only hope, and on this hope I hang every other thing in this life. To learn that the exchange I have long toiled and strived for has already taken place is a greater cause for celebration than anything else in this life.

Spirit Surrender

Even though I know so much truth, I am a wretched man, driven to do things daily which are not consistent with Your truth, oh God! The spirit man inside me is desperately trying to come out, to break through this outer shell, these powerful layers that harness and drive and control my spirit, when it should be the other way around.

I have come to learn that my soul is my spirit's worst enemy, and likewise, my body is my soul's worst enemy. This body of flesh is what allows me to be a vessel for holiness, for light, for purity, for truth— and yet the very thing You desire to use for your purposes is the one thing that resists and rebels and puts up the greatest fight as I journey toward a place of submission, as I move closer to a life of obedience, as I come to know and experience the meaning of the word *surrender*.

To surrender my body to my soul and my soul to my spirit— that will be the end of all my striving. That will be the laying down of my own wants and desires, the end of my very will. That will be the death of me. And what a glorious day, that day of death, for it opens the door to resurrection— it paves the way to life. The death of who I thought I was will be the very birth of who I truly am.

Breaths are growing shallow. Eyes are closing. My grip is loosening. Death is knocking on my door— and I welcome it with gratitude, for I already know the glory that comes when the stone is rolled away.

Something Better

We will always struggle with habitual sin in our lives until we are convinced that there is something better than the sin we keep committing.

To do our best to resist and stand our ground and stay strong in the face of temptation— this alone is not enough. Willpower will not do it. Determination cannot pluck us out of the grip of bondage.

It is only when grace is granted us to set our sight on something so much better, something of far greater value than the worthless thing we have become preoccupied with, that we can begin to move forward.

We should not think of it as a journey away from sin, but rather a journey toward God and into the purposes He has for us. As we travel toward God and move closer to His heart, deeper into His will for us, we will at the same time be naturally moving away from the things that hold no value for us in His kingdom, the things that are not written on His heart or a part of His will.

So it is not a frustration with our sin, with our own waywardness, that will drive us to complete abandonment of it, but a passion for something far grander.

It is in catching a glimpse of the splendor and the glory of God, the magnitude of His purposes and the incredible ways in which He has woven each of us into these purposes, that will pull us away from lesser things. But our desire for worthless and sinful things will only decrease as our desire for something else increases.

The more we know and understand and experience God, the less enamored with sin we will become. So instead of focusing on getting rid of the worthless things that fill our lives, we should focus on God and how great He is. And as our eyes truly begin to be opened to the reality of our awesome, eternal, glorious God, we will find temporary and fleeting things begin to fade away and drop off. We will only forsake the sin once we have learned to be satisfied by God instead.

For Only You

Watch the snow falling outside,
let it pile light and high
on the doorstep,
the hood of the car,
the naked branches.

Watch it come down
in tentative swells and mountains,
and know that the next season
will be all clean and white
and forgiving
like a five course meal prepared just for you,
like a gown set aside for this one occasion,
a gift saved for your eyes only.

Know that it will be young
and virgin
and full of possibility
and that you won't be able
to believe
or refuse it
when it comes calling.

Press your face to the window
and take it,
let it swirl around you
and don't despise it.
Let the new thing come
and know that you are undeserving;
let yourself be humble and glad
under a generous sky.

Know that something will sprout up
from under that melted brown and white mess,
and that it will be a good thing,

a strong and sure thing
for you to sit and swing under.

Know that it will come in the waiting
the same way you wait for the water to boil,
the phone to ring,
and the sickness to leave your body.

Know that it will come in time,
in perfect time,
and know that it will be much bigger
than it appears at first—
bigger and much, much taller
than the picture in your little mind.

Let it grow, give it space and light,
and let it be more than you imagined,
more than you dreamed,

more than your folded hands and closed eyes
could have thought to ask for.

When the joy does finally find you,
take it in your arms
like a newborn babe,
look it full in the eye and know
that you will not forsake it
because it came here for you,

for only you.

God in Nature

Oh Sun, how I love you!
Your warmth; your beauty
Your unfailing consistency
Reach me with your rays;
Burn me through and through
Lift me from these dark depths
So I might never again have to feel
This alone
This cold
Please deliver me now

Oh Wind, how I long for you!
For your lack of predictability
For your sense of wonder
Your invisibility
Your ability to move worlds
Oh Wind, come move in me now
Stir in me something new
Change these intentions
Break these stubborn hands
Heal my bones and bind my wounds
Carry me over to the other side
To a better place
A place I know so little of—
a much better place

Oh mighty Sea, how you amaze me;
Your strength, your capacity!
The way you come and go in waves and tides
In gentleness and insistence
Each and every day
In time, in season
Following the rhythm of the Sun and the moon,
Obeying the commands of the Wind and the rain
Your shades of blue and green reflecting passions and emotions

Buried deep within my salty soul
Behind my face stained with tears
Beyond the wisdom of my years

Oh God, what can I say?
You amaze me more every day!
Your strength, your beauty
Your passion and ingenuity
Shown through your creation
Displayed throughout the world
Given to me in the form of nature
To be seen and enjoyed,
To be found and known
Just as you long to be known, oh God
I beg of you: Know me
Let our hearts always be one
Know me more!
Let me know you equally well
Let us spend an eternity in union
Intimate
Mirrored
As one

Once In A Life

Once in a life
Destiny reaches out its hand
To open up your mind
And make you understand
To take you to a place
Where you have never been before
And lay you down to sleep
Where you will want no more

Once in a life
Dreams have a chance at coming true
They often come in the form of something
That seems so very foreign to you
But as long as you recognize them
And claim them as your own
After the flowers have all withered
What matters most to you will stand proud like stone

Once in a life
Time just stands still
For a little pause,
a thread of eternity
Just for a moment
Giving you time to drink your fill
Of everything you long for, before your life is spent

Oak of Splendor

this is how you have grown me—
slowly and painfully and precisely

i labor under the weight of your glory
while you remain outside time
seeing the oak of splendor in me

The Water Will Settle

after all your tears
have come down

the river, washed
into the salty sea

collected in the
ocean of all that

shouldn't be,
in layers of regret

and second guessing:
the water will settle.

you will come to
rest, your ark

secure on ararat.
you will stand

on a mountain
all your own.

you will cultivate
it, give it a fence,

boundaries, and
a name—

after the glacier
of fire that smolders

inside your soul
has found its way

down the mountain,
after the ice has

burned into clear
liquid, there at

the bottom: *the
water will settle.*

you will find a
peaceful current

to sail upon.
you will feel the

wind in your face
under clouds that

cannot threaten
or harm you any

longer. you will
cast your nets on

the other side
and bring back

more harvest than
your baskets can

hold. you will lay
on banks in safety

as tides rise and
fall around you.

after the storm
has had its way

with you, after
the trees have

fallen, after the
morning dew has

been left alone
to lay on tender

blades of grass,
after all things

have wound their
way down, have

found their place,
floated under the

bridge in twilight:
the water will settle.

Legacy

Tears are the torture
released in the pain
little reminders
of a life gone insane

Fear is the flesh
that rips and tears
and covers itself
in dismal despair

Lies are the language
spoken by the shamed
desperately grasping
for a better name

Death is the demon
that taunts your mind
refusing to let you leave
those memories behind

Hope is a hand
that reaches out
and does its best
to understand

Freedom is a feather
that glides and soars
on tomorrow's wind
seeking something more

Grace is a garment
that covers all stain
refreshing and renewing
like a cleansing rain

Love is a legacy
leaving behind
glimpses of eternity
for the faithful to find

To Have Won

Not to be, but to become
Not to fight, but to overcome
Not to think, but to create
Not to describe, but to illustrate

Not to wonder, but to know
Not to tell, but to show
Not to whisper, but to say
Not to speak, but to convey

Not to plant, but to grow
Not to stay, but to go
Not to do, but to have done
Not to struggle, but to have won

Hope

Uninspired. If I am completely honest with myself or anyone else, I have to admit that this is exactly how I've been feeling lately. Unmotivated. Lifeless. Recklessly suspended. Aimlessly wandering—toward what? I'm not even sure.

There have been times when inspiration rushed in, meeting my soul, flooding me with hope, allowing me to rise to such heights that nothing under the sun could tame my passion. Days when my lips have been dripping with praise, flowing with gratitude at the knowledge of the grace that has been extended to me.

Then when the rain and wind find me again, all I know to do is fold myself up, sit shivering with my head at my knees, waiting for the storm to pass, and longing for the sun to shine down on me bright and beautiful again. For some reason I always put up such a resistance to the storms, forgetting that they are inevitable, and even more so necessary for growth and success.

Looking out the window this morning, I was suddenly reminded of this simple truth as I stared at a tree. Lifeless, for the most part, by its appearance. No leaves hung from its branches. Its once vibrant and shiny skin looked more weathered and beaten than ever before. Instead of standing tall and proud with arms outstretched, this tree seemed rather to be huddled as close to the ground as possible, its face hung in shame, trying to maintain what little it had left to speak of.

And then it hit me. This tree goes through this very same thing every year. I'm sure it doesn't even fight it anymore. In fact, it probably expects it by now. Every year when its leaves begin to change color, adorning the tree with brilliant beauty, the tree must be smiling bittersweetly to itself, because the tree knows that after the glory fades and its leaves are blown to the ground by the harsh wind, the hardest season is coming.

And yet the tree smiles anyway, because it knows the value of the changing seasons. It knows that in order for any growth to take place in the coming year, it must first be humbled and defaced, beaten and brought low to the ground, stripped bare and left out in the cold for a time.

I remember looking at this same tree a few months ago when I first moved here, and marveling at its impressive height, its strong branches, and vibrant green, inviting leaves. You would hardly recognize it now. But looking at it even now, this tree is still beautiful to me.

I can't wait for springtime to come, so I can clap my hands and rejoice with the tree as it peeks the first white buds from behind its fresh coat of skin. And if I am here long enough, I will watch the tree go from white to green, to yellow to orange and red, and then completely bare again.

Looking at this tree, I am humbled and inspired, as I make the obvious connection to my own life. I, too, live in a world of constantly changing seasons. I, like the tree, know how it feels to stand naked and humbled, hanging my face in shame until the new year brings me to life again with the promise of spring.

We have been talking a lot lately about hope. The word has been on my mind a lot, and I've tried again and again to define it for myself and figure out what it means. Sitting here on this cold dark winter morning, with this lifeless tree as my only witness, for the first time in awhile, I have hope again.

I feel foolish for not realizing it sooner. These seasons were meant for me. I was not set into motion to exist in a constant state and stay the same forever. So rather than fight the changing of the seasons, I should embrace them gratefully, because I, like the tree, have come to learn the value of enduring hardship because I know that growth will inevitably follow.

Looking at the tree, I don't see hope. There is no evidence at all suggesting that there is any hope at all for this pathetic tree. But even though I do not see hope, I feel it, and better yet, I know it exists, and I believe that the tree, just like me, will come to life again.

It is not dancing on the branches or shouting out loud. It is subtle. It is concealed. It is laying low behind the scenes. It takes some faith sometimes to believe in. But it is there—and it's called hope.

Morning Prayer

Oh great God,
I fear that I am
getting away from You again

Come with your hands,
strong and wise
and hedge me in
the way only You can

Come with your gaze,
eternal and deep,
and capture me
the way only your eyes do

Come with your discipline,
gentle and firm,
and move the lesser things
out of me once more

Come with your love,
perfectly painted,
and remind me of grace
again

Walking Away

I have come to learn that walking away from your past is not like stepping out of your house, closing the door behind you and heading out down the street. No, it is much more like being tethered to the house by an invisible rubber leash, one that allows you to progress only a limited few steps from the house before attempting to pull you back. Anyone who has ever tried to leave their past behind knows very well what I am talking about.

They know how easy it can seem at first, setting your direction and forming a plan, and taking that first step in complete confidence that the future is easily attainable, and everything they hope for awaits them on a new horizon. They also know the all too familiar tug of the leash after the first few steps are taken. They can relate to the constant nagging and tugging that becomes so strong that at times it seems difficult, or even impossible, to take the next step without falling flat on your face, or worse yet, bouncing right back to where you started, only to sit on your doorstep and wonder if it's even worth it, if you should even stand back up and try again.

Many of us have tried time and time again to get rid of this leash. Some of us have even thought at times that maybe we had gotten free, that there was nothing hindering our steps or holding us back anymore. So we begin to skip along, effortless and carefree, only to fall down again because we weren't paying attention or watching our steps.

I am ashamed to admit that I have been through this cycle myself countless times; and even more ashamed to admit that there have been times when I went back to the house willingly, even when I wasn't feeling a strong tug on my leash; moments of despair and disillusionment when I became afraid of this new horizon and decided it would be safer and far more comfortable to go back and spend another night at my old house, before reassessing the situation and gathering up the courage to set out on my journey again.

There are two things we know for sure; the first is that there is a journey marked out for us that will lead us to a much better place; and the second is that we will never get anywhere by staying in this house, or by lingering in the front yard. If we have admitted to ourselves and to others that this place we have been living is not where we want to stay, then it would only make sense for us to do whatever we can to get as far away as we can from our old house.

But unfortunately, the fear of the unknown often paralyzes our faith and causes us to waste so much precious time while we pace back and forth on our leash and think about the house we wish we lived in; a house with three stories, a big porch and a swimming pool, surrounded by beautiful gardens and trees; a house we have heard about and have seen only in our wildest dreams. None of us would ever deny that we want to live in a house like that; but we must first believe it exists before we set out to find it.

All this time of wandering around my yard and dreaming about the house I hope to live in someday has given me a lot of time to think. And I have realized that the decision to walk away from something is not a decision that is made only once. It is a decision that has to be made every single day, every moment even.

We wake up, our feet hit the floor, and we make the decision to keep on walking. Sometimes we don't know what direction we're supposed to be going, how far the road is going to stretch in front of us, or exactly where it is going to lead even; but we keep on walking anyway; and that is the most important thing for us to remember, is that we have to keep walking. When the sweat and tears fill our eyes and we can't even see, we have to keep on walking. When it seems that everyone else has abandoned us and we are the only one walking down this road, we have to keep on walking. When the darkness sets in and the street lights are all burnt out, we have to keep on walking. When the blisters on our feet are screaming for a rest, for some form of relief, we have to keep on walking.

And one day, probably when we least expect it, we will pause to look back and see just how far we've come. The dirty little house whose walls seemed to haunt and imprison us at one time will start to fade from our view, and yes, even from our memory, as we keep on walking.

The leash, though it may never be completely cut off, loses its power over us as time passes, to the point where we may hardly even notice it anymore, and probably only feel its pull occasionally; and when we do, we don't let it stop us, because we know its tricks and have learned to bend against the pressure, and we have come too far to think of turning back; and because this time we know where we are headed, and have made up our minds to get there, even if it takes the rest of our lives.

I have heard it said that the journey of a thousand miles begins with a single step. The key is to take that first step and decide every moment of every day that you are not going to look back, because that would just be foolish. You already know that you can't live in this house anymore, so there's no point in staying another night.

And when you're waiting for the street lights to come on and wondering when the blisters on your feet are going to stop throbbing, when you're doing your best to resist the pull of your leash and wondering how much longer you have to hang on, just close your eyes and think about the big house with the porch and the swimming pool, and keep on walking.

I Said / She Said

I said: How's your heart?
She said: It's broken apart.

I said: Show me the pieces.
She said: What good will that do?

I said: I can take them to Jesus for you.
She said: There's too many pieces.

I said: There's never too many pieces for Him.
She said: I can't let go.

I said: Just open up your hands and let me take them from you.
She said: What are you going to do with them?

I said: I'm going to give them to Jesus.
She said: How long will it take?

I said: The sooner you let go the sooner you'll get your heart back.
She said: OK

I said: Do you trust me?
She said: I do.

I said: Where's your heart now?
She said: It's in Jesus' hands.

I said: That's the best place for it.
She said: I'm afraid

I said: I think you're brave
She said: I'm going to close my eyes now

I said: When you open them again
Jesus will give you back your heart.
She said: He already did. But this isn't my heart.

I said: It is now.
She said: This is a brand new heart.

I said: I know.
She said: Why?

I said: Because He loves you.
She said: How?

I said: He just does.
She said: I have nothing to say.

I said: How's your heart now?
She said: It's beautiful. How's yours?

I said: It's broken apart.
She said: Show me the pieces.

I said: What good will that do?
She said: I can take them to Jesus for you.

Sadness

There is the sadness that comes to you
like the prick of a pin
when you are in a room full of people
and you feel suddenly alone;
the kind that sits
like a restless bird on your shoulder
or a cold stone in your hand.

There is the sadness
that bears its weight
from the inside of you,
rises up out of your very bones
and settles over you
heavy and insistent,
bringing with it the feeling of dread
that you know you will try to shake.
Oh, how you know it!

You will try and try
and it may be days
or weeks
before it leaves you alone again;
a residual stalker,
a well enforced habit
that refuses to be buried
while it still has breath.

Then there is a sadness
that will break over you
like a crushing wave,
too big for you to ride,
too quick for you to anticipate—
the kind of sadness that you will
give yourself to
and claim as your own

because you remember this sadness:

the way it took your hand
and led you out of despair,
away from hopelessness
into a place where tears are welcomed
and brokenness is allowed.

It is in the quiet, clean
breaking of that sadness,
the voluntary splitting of yourself
into parts
that you will come to see
and know yourself as whole.

Little Mountains

My lack of discipline shows itself
gradually but faithfully
in the folds of skin that collect
around my middle,
in my unkept kitchen,
in the letter laying
half written upon my desk,
in friendships void of love,
slowly deteriorating and
pulling apart
one selfish motive at a time;

in the excuses,
the half truths,
in the little piles of dust
that I step over each day,
the tiny piles that move
themselves into the
convenient corners of my life
and threaten to become mountains.

He Said To Me

I'm glad for love,
so grateful for it.

I'm glad that love
has nothing to do
with anything else.

I don't understand
you. I don't agree
with you.

But I love you.

Falling

I got so high on what I thought was real—
hung my hat on the only dream that
ever made sense to me.

So when I fell from that dream,
I fell long and hard.

I guess I'm still falling. I guess I haven't
hit the ground quite yet.

Please

Soften my heart, Lord,
Soften my heart

Even in the places
where I still want stones

Even in the places
I have made my own—

Soften it, Lord Jesus

You Are

You are not in a box
You are not on a page
You are everlasting comfort
You are the same from age to age

You are not a church
You are not a denomination
You are eternal life
You are the gift of salvation

You are not a picture
You are not a song
You are my new blessing every morning
You are my valiant warrior, tall and strong

You are not limited
You are not contained
You are everywhere at once
You run wild and unchained

You are not what they say you are
You are not what they make of you
You are God, one and only
You are God, tried and true

You are not who I thought you were
You are not where I thought you would be
You are God, my friend and deliverer
You are God, living inside of me

more

the more of
You
i give away
the more
beautiful
You
become to
me

the more of
Your life
that i share
with others
the more
alive
i become

for you

if you find in my eyes
deep wells of sorrow
know that they have been dug with deep conviction
carved out of the passion that flows from my Saving Grace—
and know that they are overflowing for you

if you find in my voice
words of life and power and light
know that they have been crafted with careful consideration
born out of the overflow of
the things my forgiving Jesus has spoken to me;
and know that they are calling out for you

if you find in my actions and intentions
something of value and beauty
know that they have been unleashed
from the power of redemption
built by each step my Master has led me down;
and know that they testify for you

if you find in my song
a melody to pierce your soul
know that the tune i dance to is not my own,
that it flows from the River of Life planted deep inside me;
and know that the same River is singing for you

if you find in my soul
anything good or praiseworthy at all
know that i am a ray of light that was once deep darkness,
drawn from the pit by an offer of Exchange;
and know that the same Exchange is waiting for you

if you find in my prayers
a Faith to move mountains
know that i am a child of the valley,

that i have seen the dry bones come back to Life;
and know that a mountain is moving for you

if you find in my eyes a Fire burning bright and bold
know that this Fire is named Love,
that i can only give what i have received;
and know that this Fire is burning for you

Praying for Perseverance

Freedom is a place not
so far away for you, my friend—

it is a place just on the other
side of this wall—

but it is a very thick wall,
and it will take a very
solid faith to penetrate it.

Impartation

When you hugged me
you squeezed out the last two years
and put your love inside instead.

When you spoke to me
your words cut away some shame
and made room for faith.

When you looked at my face
heaven came and sat on my shoulder,
grace reached out of nowhere
for my hand…

In My Own Words

Hebrews 12:1-13

I have so many people rooting for me and cheering me on-- I think it's time to leave the past behind me, and free myself from all distractions so I can actually engage myself in this race once and for all.

The most important thing I need to remember as I run is to not look away from Jesus' face, but keep gazing more and more intently at Him, keeping in mind that He's the One who makes this whole thing possible, from the beginning to the end. He invited me into this journey of faith, and He will see me through to the very last mile until I arrive safely at home. I need to remember too that Jesus also ran this same race I'm running now, and because He was so focused on the bigger picture and so thrilled to do what His Father asked Him to, He didn't let anything bother Him-- even being put to death-- because He knew that His Father was already waiting for Him and had reserved the most special seat for Him in Heaven.

When I think about Jesus and all that He went through, it motivates me to keep pressing on and not give up. Sometimes I feel like my struggles are really hard-- but compared to what Jesus went through for me, my hard times really aren't that bad at all.

How often have I forgotten this command: "My Son, don't resist Your Heavenly Father when He tries to correct and rebuke you, because your Heavenly Father only does this to those children He loves, and if He considers you a true Son, He will let you know when He is not pleased with you."

So I'll just look at the hard times as lessons I get to learn. God is taking the time to teach me because I am His Son and He loves me.

What Dad wouldn't want to pass on valuable things to His kids? If my Dad didn't discipline me (and everyone gets disciplined once in awhile) then I would question whether He really loved me as a son.

My Dad disciplined me and raised me the best he knew how, and after I grew up, I came to love and respect him for it. It would make sense then that God would do the same thing, and I should be glad to receive it, because I know His instruction is paving the way for me to have a good, fruitful life. And I have to remember that God cuts off the rotten parts of me only because He wants me to be pure and flawless, like He is.

Discipline is never fun when we are receiving it, but afterwards it brings about so many good and necessary things in us that it is definitely more than worth it.

So knowing all of this, I am going to stand up straight and exercise my spiritual muscles a little, because I don't want to see the hopeless sink even deeper into the dark-- I want to let God speak through me so they will know that there is hope and healing, and that they can come out of their beds and walk around without wheelchairs or crutches.

revival

revival
is not a city
a place
a skyline
or a structure
it is
a person
a face
a heart
a name
it is a little tiny spark
burning a little tiny flame
that starts slowly
and softly
but grows as far as it is willed
by the one who carries it
willingly

revival
is not forced
is not imagined
or charted
it is conceived
grown
and birthed
by a man, a woman
a father, a mother
whose children stand speaking
in their womb
words that will be heard
for eternity to come

revival
does not begin
in cleveland

in chicago
in new york
or atlanta
it begins
anytime
any place
where a fire is allowed to burn
it begins
on the coldest
darkest night
on the inside
of someone looking outside
with a faith like a candle
and a voice just like the wind
someone who has allowed themselves
to be devastated
only to be
built back up again

revival
begins
inside of you
inside of me
it has a definite beginning
but no end
for things that grow
never stop
things that carry life inside
never die
cannot be put out
put down
or laid to rest

revival
does not stand on top of a mountain
it lies dormant in
a single grain of sand

it sleeps unsuspectingly
in a word
a phrase
an ounce of truth
that waits like a virgin land
to be discovered
for the first time
by one who will step
outside their world
outside their box
outside their reputation
into a dimension
that laughs at three
and weeps for sunday mornings
carried by a melody
that can only be heard
by humble ears
ears that know
and acknowledge
that they do not know

'revival...'
you say
and that is your first mistake
that is the tragedy you carry
and wear on your sleeve
your tragedy is your posture
the way you sit
the way you stand
the way you run
as if revival is something
you can walk to
or drive to
or climb high enough to reach

revival
is coming to those who wait

to the broken
and beat up
to the lost
and shamed
to the prostitute at his feet
to the woman with a bucket
she can never fill
to the fragmented
who know they need a thread
to weave them back together
to those
who are ready
and willing
to jump
to let go
at just the right moment
when the time is right
to lose everything

when you finally realize
that you can't
but believe
that he can
when you shout 'amen'
and whisper under your breath
'to hell with it'
that is when
revival
will come to you again

Let It Shine

I have learned painstakingly that
you don't have to work hard
at pushing the darkness away

Work instead at cultivating your light
and letting it shine
brighter and brighter

and the darkness will eventually
either go away, or be changed by your light—

It will either run from it
or embrace it
It will be offended by it
or inspired by it

Your only job is to
keep shining your light

Gospel Gifts

You gave me Peter to remind me
that sometimes we fail the very worst
right before we win

You gave me John to remind me
that it's OK to lean on your shoulder
and let You wash my feet

You gave me Thomas to remind me
that even when I am faithless,
You move through walls,
through time and space
to show yourself faithful

You gave me Nicodemus to remind me
that sometimes I just have to
get alone with You
and ask You the right questions

Easy

I'm glad it's not easy,
because easy does not make

good movies,
good money,
or good men.

Easy is a heavier weight
to bear than it seems.

The satisfaction of resolution
after the torturous trial of
conflict is what I really want
because that is what makes a good
story, a good ending a good
life for you and me.

Underneath

As high as the branches,
so deep are the roots

Every time God wants to
lift you up higher,
He must first dig you deeper—

Not for punishment,
but for mercy
Not for pain,
but for support

Before the exalting,
the humbling—
Before the eager shouting
from the rooftops,
the dark mumbling underneath;

Before the harvest,
the heavy whispering inside the earth…

Wanderings of a Son

I see Eve standing in front of a tree
Her mouth is watering; she wants to know more
Strangely enough, she is a lot like me
For I have been caught standing in that very same place before

I see Joseph persevering, resisting temptation
Always doing what he knows is best
I am being offered that same salvation
But so often I insist on failing the test

I see Jonah running as fast as he can
Disobeying God, for he is scared to death
I too have been running just like that man
Stumbling in my own sin, gasping for each breath

I have been so wrong
I have wandered so far
I am not worthy of anyone's love
And yet…

I see a shepherd leaving the ninety-nine
To seek out and find the one that is lost
I weep at knowing that one heart is mine
But the shepherd says, "Nothing is too great a cost…"

I see a table and a feast,
A place of honor reserved just for me
I sense the present of ten thousand angels
Welcoming me to eternity

I finally see His face and hear His voice
Speaking the words, "Well done…"
My head drops: *"I can't believe He still loves me;*
I can't believe He just called me His son."

I reach out and touch the hands that bled for me
And I realize for the first time the price love chooses to pay
I look into the eyes that for my sake have wept in agony
Though my mouth does not move, my tears have much to say

Opportunity

What few humble apologies separate
the healthy from the broken—
what very few moments of admitting
that we're wrong
divide the foolish from the wise

What few kind words, spoken in perfect time
separate the praised from the rejected—
how very short the road is
from dismayed to overjoyed

How subtle the fears that assume power
with eager suggestion and convince us
to lose when we've already won

What few stitches it takes
to sew a heart closed,
what few neglectful turns of the head
make the familiar distant strangers

How unassuming the bits of pride
that come in and dig up what we have sown,
tear down what we have built—
and how easily we let that pride in!

What tiny bits of discipline,
what minuscule difference lies between
the frustrated and the successful

What simple, honest, deliberate prayers

lift the dying from their graves

What small open doors invite
the lonely to become loved,
to join a family all their own,
to sit in a place of honor

What tiny fragments of light
through a single window
can warm an entire house
and rebuke the shadows until
they are standing silent in the corner

What little effort of the will it takes
to be different, to make a difference

How often opportunities come knocking
and how quick we are
to close the shutters
and lock the doors

How close life breathes on us
and how often we hold our breath,
turn our heads
and close our eyes
just long enough to miss it

Hands and Feet

The hours you spent with me
They were the legs, you see
that stood up and walked with me
The arms that carried me
The hands that took mine and said
"there is a much better place for you"
Then your eyes looked and saw for me
and helped me to believe

The words you spoke to me
They were the grace, you see
that came and wrapped itself around me
They became the bread on my table
the logs on my fire
the blankets on my bed—
sometimes the starving
just need a few bites,
a few minutes in front of the flame,
a few hours of free rest

The things you did for me
and the ways you served me,
they were the dots
in my color by number, you see
They were the bones on my form
that gave me shape
until I could find enough ink
to make it come to life,
until I could gather enough mortar
to fill in the gaps

and fit into all the spaces

The prayers you prayed for me
when I wasn't looking
They were the walls, you see
That built this house I live in now
Your tears became the foundation
Your conviction the cornerstones
Your faith the solid doorposts
that guard me as I come in and out

Your silent cries in the night
brought forth the lumber
Your aching at dawn
beckoned the angels in flight
Your commitment to truth
forged the key to fit perfectly in my chains

I guess what I'm trying to say is,
I understand now: that when
Jesus said we are his body,
his mouthpiece,
his hands and his feet—

He was talking about you

Never Alone

When I see the warm glow
of yellow light
turn the corner into the driveway

When I hear the soft shuffling
of tired feet on the stairs,
the turning and creaking and
fitting of the door into its place

When the steam rises
tall and generous from the plate,
the bowl, and the cup set before me

I know at last
that I am not alone—

and remember at last
that I never was

Morning Star

The hours of early morning
are multiplied in silence

The dawn, an easy highway
for travelers few and far—

The daybreak, a bed of treasures
for patient, deliberate digging;

The slumber, a small price to pay
for the wishing of a Morning Star

Channels

What a glorious moment
when you find that
your darkest secrets
and strangest longings
are not uncommon,
but relatable;
not shameful,
but inspiring—

When you find that
the valleys and trenches
are not low places,
not empty places of want,
but channels to carry
all that is coming down
from the mountains
to the sea

What a humble moment
when you find that the digging
was for someone else—
that the pain, it laid the bricks
and forged a path to pave the way
from death to life

What a moment it is
when the Sun finally touches
your darkest places,
and you see them for what they are—

not stumbling blocks,
but stepping stones;
not graves or rotting tombs—

but seeded fields and fertile wombs

Runner

There's grace at the start,
mercy in the middle
and love, everlasting love
waiting for you at the finish line

Light Shovels

In the quiet of early morning,
we mine for truth.

While the first long legs of light
running ahead of the others
are searching for cities and mountains,
for ocean blue,
somewhere safe to touch down—

We are searching for You.

shine again

we muddy and mire the gospel
in all its strength
and purity
with our complaints
our circles
our lack of simple faith

we need this gospel
and the purity of its light
to come wash the black from our eyes
pick the brown and grey out of them
rub the scorn and anxiety from their pores
kneed the apathy and excuses
from their humble creases
so they can shine
bright and blue again
the way they were meant to
the way the world needs them to—
so they can be pathways instead of prisons,
windows instead of walls

New Mercy

You never stop working,
even in the darkness—
You don't need the sun to see.

Overnight: the digging,
the leveling, the filling
of potholes, the removing
of stones…

It's funny how the dark
becomes a holy eraser, the
blankets on my bed a
shroud of forgiveness;

my sleep a reset button
and my dreams a plea,
though there's no need to ask—

You already have new mercy waiting for me.

There's Room

There is room in my heart for you,
you see—

there's a stretcher and some ointment
and a place to rest for free.

Chambers

You gave me two hands and said
life will be a battle,
you will have to make a choice—
and then you gave me just one voice.

You gave me two ears and just as many
hemispheres and said
here's a line to divide the two because
there is one light and one dark half of you.

You gave me three: a body a soul
and a spirit, and said model yourself
after me, a holy Trinity.

You gave me four seasons,
four chambers in my heart and said
beat beat beat for me, just for me
until all of you
gives and receives my blood,
my life, my words and my ways.

You said love me with all of your
heart soul mind and strength
until not one, not two, not even three—

but all four parts of you beat for me.

Sing

Sing in four dimensions
so we can know the love he spoke of

Sing again until that love is falling from the ceiling
the height of it
the breadth
the length—

yes, even the depth
because we need all four walls around us

If God was a house
His love would sit square
with an extra horizon
on a hillside

Sing again, and let your song
be the light
in the window
that calls us
home

Additional thanks to…

Ed and Traci Munoz for being my spiritual parents and giving me a foundation to grow from

Nick, Adrienne, Sarah, and Lydia Poelking for being my home away from home

Ryan Hutton for putting up with me, challenging me and being a blast at the same time

Reid Phifer and Todd Calaway for open arms and hearts

Ashley Baker for constant prayer, encouragement, inspiration, and loyal love. You were right beside me during the birth of most of these writings— they are just as much yours as they are mine

The majority of these confessions

came to being in:

Orlando, Florida

The rest were voiced and written in:

Camdenton, Missouri

Port Angeles, Washington

Cleveland, Ohio

RUSS BRUNN was born and raised in the island nation of Papua New Guinea and has enjoyed writing poems and short stories since childhood.

Since graduating from high school he has lived in California, Florida, Missouri, and now makes his home in Cleveland, Ohio where he is pursuing a Creative Writing degree at Cleveland State University.

Brunn's other hobbies include gardening, cooking, traveling, reading, and playing piano. You can find him on facebook or write to him at russpng84@yahoo.com.

More copies of this book may be

purchased on Amazon.com

Also available from Russ Brunn:

First and Second Person

a collection of poems

Made in the USA
Charleston, SC
28 October 2013